Cooking with Kids: 50 Fun and Easy Recipes

By: Kelly Johnson

Table of Contents

- Mini Pizza Pockets
- Fruit Salad Kabobs
- Homemade Chicken Tenders
- Banana Pancakes
- No-Bake Energy Bites
- Veggie Quesadillas
- DIY Trail Mix
- Chocolate Chip Cookie Dough Bites
- Mini Tacos
- Apple Nachos
- Chocolate-Dipped Strawberries
- Grilled Cheese Sandwiches
- Sweet Potato Fries
- Fruit Popsicles
- Mini Muffins
- DIY Pita Chips
- Smoothie Bowls
- DIY Pizza with Fresh Toppings
- Homemade Granola Bars
- Veggie Sticks with Hummus
- Chocolate-Covered Pretzels
- Apple Sandwiches with Peanut Butter
- Mini Pancake Stacks
- Veggie and Cheese Skewers
- Fun Sandwich Faces
- Frozen Yogurt Bark
- Mac and Cheese Cups
- Fruit and Yogurt Parfaits
- Mini Frittatas
- Cinnamon Roll Bites
- Mini Calzones
- Carrot and Cucumber Rolls
- Egg Salad Sandwiches
- Frozen Banana Bites
- Rice Cake Snacks

- Cheese and Crackers Art
- Veggie Pancakes
- Breakfast Burritos
- Apple Cinnamon Oatmeal
- Chocolate Rice Krispies Treats
- DIY Ice Cream Cones
- Homemade Pudding Cups
- Pita Bread Pizzas
- Fruit and Cheese Kabobs
- Sweet Potato and Apple Hash
- Spinach and Cheese Pinwheels
- Popcorn Trail Mix
- Mini Bagel Pizzas
- Fruit Smoothies
- Veggie and Cheese Muffins

Mini Pizza Pockets

Ingredients:

- 1 package refrigerated biscuit dough
- 1/2 cup pizza sauce
- 1 cup shredded mozzarella cheese
- Optional fillings: pepperoni, diced veggies, or cooked sausage
- 1 egg, beaten

Instructions:

1. Preheat oven to 375°F (190°C).
2. Roll out each biscuit into a flat circle.
3. Add a small spoonful of pizza sauce, cheese, and desired fillings to the center.
4. Fold the dough over to form a pocket and press edges to seal.
5. Brush with beaten egg and bake on a parchment-lined baking sheet for 12-15 minutes, or until golden brown.

Fruit Salad Kabobs

Ingredients:

- Assorted fresh fruits (e.g., grapes, melon, pineapple, strawberries, blueberries)
- Skewers

Instructions:

1. Thread fruits onto skewers in a colorful pattern.
2. Serve as a refreshing snack or dessert.
3. Optional: Drizzle with honey or sprinkle with powdered sugar.

Homemade Chicken Tenders

Ingredients:

- 1 lb chicken breast, cut into strips
- 1/2 cup flour
- 2 eggs, beaten
- 1 cup breadcrumbs (plain or seasoned)
- 1/2 teaspoon paprika
- Salt and pepper, to taste
- Cooking oil

Instructions:

1. Preheat oven to 400°F (200°C) or heat oil in a skillet for frying.
2. Coat chicken strips in flour, then dip in beaten eggs, and finally in breadcrumbs mixed with paprika, salt, and pepper.
3. Arrange on a baking sheet or fry until golden and cooked through.
4. Serve with dipping sauces like ketchup or ranch.

Banana Pancakes

Ingredients:

- 1 ripe banana
- 1 egg
- 1/4 cup flour
- 1/4 teaspoon baking powder
- Pinch of salt
- Butter or oil for cooking

Instructions:

1. Mash the banana in a bowl and mix with the egg.
2. Add flour, baking powder, and salt, stirring to form a batter.
3. Heat a non-stick skillet over medium heat and add butter or oil.
4. Pour small amounts of batter to make pancakes and cook for 2-3 minutes per side.
5. Serve with syrup, honey, or fresh fruit.

No-Bake Energy Bites

Ingredients:

- 1 cup oats
- 1/2 cup peanut butter
- 1/3 cup honey
- 1/4 cup chocolate chips
- 1/4 cup ground flaxseed

Instructions:

1. Combine all ingredients in a bowl and mix well.
2. Roll into bite-sized balls.
3. Chill in the refrigerator for 30 minutes before serving.

Veggie Quesadillas

Ingredients:

- 4 flour tortillas
- 1 cup shredded cheese (cheddar, Monterey Jack, or a mix)
- 1 cup diced veggies (bell peppers, onions, zucchini, or spinach)
- Cooking spray or oil

Instructions:

1. Heat a skillet over medium heat and lightly grease.
2. Place a tortilla in the skillet, sprinkle with cheese and veggies, then top with another tortilla.
3. Cook for 2-3 minutes on each side until golden and the cheese is melted.
4. Slice into wedges and serve with salsa or sour cream.

DIY Trail Mix

Ingredients:

- 1 cup mixed nuts (almonds, cashews, peanuts)
- 1/2 cup dried fruit (raisins, cranberries, or apricots)
- 1/4 cup chocolate chips or M&Ms
- 1/4 cup seeds (pumpkin or sunflower)

Instructions:

1. Mix all ingredients in a bowl.
2. Store in an airtight container for a quick snack on the go.

Chocolate Chip Cookie Dough Bites

Ingredients:

- 1/2 cup butter, softened
- 1/2 cup brown sugar
- 1/4 cup sugar
- 1/2 teaspoon vanilla extract
- 1 cup flour (heat-treated if desired)
- 1/4 cup milk
- 1/2 cup mini chocolate chips

Instructions:

1. Cream together butter, brown sugar, and sugar.
2. Mix in vanilla, flour, and milk until combined.
3. Fold in chocolate chips.
4. Roll into small balls and chill in the refrigerator for 20 minutes before serving.

Mini Tacos

Ingredients:

- 12 mini taco shells
- 1/2 lb ground beef (or chicken)
- 1/4 onion, finely chopped
- 1/2 cup shredded cheddar cheese
- 1/4 cup sour cream
- 1/4 cup salsa
- 1/4 cup chopped lettuce
- 1/4 cup diced tomatoes
- 1/4 cup jalapeño slices (optional)

Instructions:

1. Heat a skillet over medium heat and cook the ground beef and onion until browned. Season with salt, pepper, and taco seasoning (optional).
2. Warm the mini taco shells in the oven according to package instructions.
3. Assemble the mini tacos by filling each shell with the cooked beef, then topping with cheese, sour cream, salsa, lettuce, tomatoes, and jalapeños if desired.
4. Serve immediately as a fun appetizer or snack.

Apple Nachos

Ingredients:

- 2 apples, thinly sliced
- 1/4 cup peanut butter (or almond butter)
- 1/4 cup chocolate chips (optional)
- 1/4 cup granola
- 1 tablespoon honey
- 1 tablespoon mini marshmallows (optional)

Instructions:

1. Arrange the apple slices on a serving platter.
2. Microwave the peanut butter for 20-30 seconds to soften it, then drizzle it over the apple slices.
3. Sprinkle with chocolate chips, granola, mini marshmallows, and a drizzle of honey.
4. Serve immediately and enjoy this sweet and healthy treat!

Chocolate-Dipped Strawberries

Ingredients:

- 1 lb fresh strawberries, washed and dried
- 8 oz dark chocolate or milk chocolate, chopped
- 2 tablespoons coconut oil or vegetable oil

Instructions:

1. Line a baking sheet with parchment paper.
2. Melt the chocolate and oil in a heatproof bowl over a double boiler or microwave in 30-second intervals, stirring in between, until smooth.
3. Dip each strawberry into the melted chocolate, coating about two-thirds of the berry.
4. Place the dipped strawberries on the prepared baking sheet and refrigerate for 20-30 minutes until the chocolate hardens.
5. Serve chilled.

Grilled Cheese Sandwiches

Ingredients:

- 4 slices of bread
- 2 tablespoons butter, softened
- 2 slices of cheddar cheese (or cheese of your choice)
- Optional fillings: tomato slices, bacon, ham, or avocado

Instructions:

1. Butter one side of each slice of bread.
2. Place one slice of cheese on the unbuttered side of two slices of bread. Add any optional fillings, if desired.
3. Top with the remaining slices of bread, buttered side out.
4. Heat a skillet over medium heat and cook the sandwiches for 3-4 minutes on each side, until golden brown and the cheese is melted.
5. Slice and serve immediately.

Sweet Potato Fries

Ingredients:

- 2 medium sweet potatoes, peeled and cut into fries
- 2 tablespoons olive oil
- 1/2 teaspoon paprika
- 1/2 teaspoon garlic powder
- Salt and pepper to taste

Instructions:

1. Preheat the oven to 425°F (220°C).
2. Toss the sweet potato fries in olive oil, paprika, garlic powder, salt, and pepper.
3. Spread the fries in a single layer on a baking sheet.
4. Bake for 25-30 minutes, flipping halfway through, until crispy and golden.
5. Serve hot with ketchup or your favorite dipping sauce.

Fruit Popsicles

Ingredients:

- 1 1/2 cups fresh fruit (such as berries, mango, or peaches)
- 1/2 cup coconut water or fruit juice
- 1 tablespoon honey or maple syrup (optional)

Instructions:

1. Blend the fruit with coconut water or fruit juice in a blender until smooth.
2. If desired, add honey or maple syrup for sweetness.
3. Pour the mixture into popsicle molds and insert sticks.
4. Freeze for 4-6 hours or until completely frozen.
5. Run warm water over the outside of the molds to easily release the popsicles. Serve immediately.

Mini Muffins

Ingredients:

- 1 1/2 cups all-purpose flour
- 1/2 cup sugar
- 1/2 teaspoon baking soda
- 1/4 teaspoon baking powder
- 1/4 teaspoon salt
- 1/2 cup milk
- 1/4 cup vegetable oil
- 1 egg
- 1/2 teaspoon vanilla extract
- Optional add-ins: chocolate chips, blueberries, or nuts

Instructions:

1. Preheat the oven to 350°F (175°C) and line a mini muffin tin with paper liners.
2. In a bowl, mix together the flour, sugar, baking soda, baking powder, and salt.
3. In another bowl, whisk together the milk, vegetable oil, egg, and vanilla extract.
4. Combine the wet ingredients with the dry ingredients and stir until just combined. Add any optional add-ins.
5. Spoon the batter into the muffin tin, filling each cup about 2/3 full.
6. Bake for 10-12 minutes or until a toothpick inserted into the center comes out clean.
7. Let cool before serving.

DIY Pita Chips

Ingredients:

- 4 pita bread rounds
- 2 tablespoons olive oil
- 1/2 teaspoon garlic powder
- 1/2 teaspoon dried oregano
- Salt to taste

Instructions:

1. Preheat the oven to 400°F (200°C).
2. Cut the pita bread into triangles.
3. Arrange the pita triangles on a baking sheet and drizzle with olive oil.
4. Sprinkle with garlic powder, oregano, and salt.
5. Bake for 8-10 minutes, or until crispy and golden brown.
6. Serve with hummus or your favorite dip.

Smoothie Bowls

Ingredients:

- 1 frozen banana
- 1/2 cup frozen berries (such as strawberries, blueberries, or raspberries)
- 1/2 cup almond milk (or milk of your choice)
- 1 tablespoon honey or maple syrup (optional)

Toppings:

- Granola
- Sliced fruits (such as kiwi, banana, or strawberries)
- Chia seeds
- Shredded coconut
- Nuts or seeds

Instructions:

1. Blend the frozen banana, frozen berries, almond milk, and honey (if using) in a blender until smooth and thick.
2. Pour the smoothie into a bowl.
3. Top with granola, sliced fruits, chia seeds, shredded coconut, or any other desired toppings.
4. Serve immediately as a refreshing and healthy snack or breakfast.

DIY Pizza with Fresh Toppings

Ingredients:

- 1 pizza dough (store-bought or homemade)
- 1/2 cup tomato sauce
- 1 1/2 cups shredded mozzarella cheese
- Fresh toppings: pepperoni, bell peppers, mushrooms, olives, onions, tomatoes, basil leaves, etc.
- Olive oil (for drizzling)

Instructions:

1. Preheat your oven to 475°F (245°C).
2. Roll out the pizza dough on a floured surface to your desired thickness.
3. Place the dough on a baking sheet or pizza stone and spread tomato sauce over the surface.
4. Sprinkle with shredded mozzarella cheese and top with your choice of fresh toppings.
5. Drizzle with olive oil and bake for 10-12 minutes, or until the crust is golden and the cheese is melted.
6. Remove from the oven, slice, and enjoy!

Homemade Granola Bars

Ingredients:

- 2 cups rolled oats
- 1/2 cup honey or maple syrup
- 1/4 cup peanut butter (or almond butter)
- 1/4 cup mini chocolate chips (optional)
- 1/2 cup dried fruit (raisins, cranberries, apricots, etc.)
- 1/4 cup chopped nuts (almonds, walnuts, etc.)
- 1/2 teaspoon vanilla extract

Instructions:

1. In a large bowl, mix together the oats, dried fruit, nuts, and chocolate chips.
2. In a saucepan over low heat, warm the honey (or maple syrup) and peanut butter until melted and smooth.

3. Remove from heat and stir in the vanilla extract.
4. Pour the wet mixture over the dry ingredients and stir to combine.
5. Line a baking pan with parchment paper and press the mixture evenly into the pan.
6. Refrigerate for at least 2 hours to set.
7. Cut into bars and store in an airtight container.

Veggie Sticks with Hummus

Ingredients:

- 1 cucumber, sliced into sticks
- 2 carrots, peeled and sliced into sticks
- 1 bell pepper, sliced into sticks
- 1 celery stalk, sliced into sticks
- 1/2 cup hummus (store-bought or homemade)

Instructions:

1. Arrange the veggie sticks (cucumber, carrots, bell pepper, celery) on a plate.
2. Serve with hummus for dipping.
3. Enjoy this healthy snack anytime!

Chocolate-Covered Pretzels

Ingredients:

- 2 cups mini pretzels
- 8 oz dark or milk chocolate, chopped
- 1 tablespoon vegetable oil (optional, to thin the chocolate)
- Sprinkles, crushed nuts, or sea salt (optional)

Instructions:

1. Melt the chocolate and oil in a heatproof bowl over a double boiler or microwave in 30-second intervals until smooth.
2. Dip each pretzel into the melted chocolate, allowing the excess to drip off.
3. Place the dipped pretzels on a parchment-lined baking sheet.

4. Optionally, sprinkle with toppings like crushed nuts, sprinkles, or sea salt.
5. Refrigerate for 30 minutes until the chocolate hardens.
6. Serve and enjoy!

Apple Sandwiches with Peanut Butter

Ingredients:

- 2 apples, cored and sliced into rounds
- 1/4 cup peanut butter (or almond butter)
- 1 tablespoon honey (optional)
- Granola or raisins (optional)

Instructions:

1. Slice the apples into rounds and remove the cores.
2. Spread a thin layer of peanut butter on one slice of apple.
3. Top with another apple slice to form a sandwich.
4. Drizzle with honey if desired and sprinkle with granola or raisins for extra crunch.
5. Serve immediately as a fun and healthy snack!

Mini Pancake Stacks

Ingredients:

- 1 cup pancake mix
- 2/3 cup milk
- 1 egg
- 1 tablespoon butter, melted
- Maple syrup, fresh berries, or whipped cream for topping

Instructions:

1. Prepare pancake batter according to the package instructions.
2. Heat a skillet over medium heat and lightly grease with butter or cooking spray.
3. Pour small circles of batter onto the skillet to form mini pancakes.
4. Cook for 1-2 minutes on each side until golden brown.
5. Stack the mini pancakes and top with syrup, fresh berries, or whipped cream.

6. Serve immediately as a fun and delicious breakfast or snack!

Veggie and Cheese Skewers

Ingredients:

- Cherry tomatoes
- Cubes of cheese (cheddar, mozzarella, or your favorite variety)
- Cucumber slices
- Bell pepper slices
- Fresh basil leaves

Instructions:

1. Thread the veggies (tomatoes, cucumber slices, bell pepper) and cheese cubes onto small skewers or toothpicks.
2. Optionally, add fresh basil leaves for extra flavor.
3. Arrange on a serving platter and serve as a healthy, fun snack or appetizer.

Fun Sandwich Faces

Ingredients:

- 2 slices of bread
- 1 tablespoon mayonnaise or cream cheese
- 2 slices of cheese
- Sliced vegetables (carrots, cucumbers, tomatoes, olives, etc.)
- 2 slices deli meat or cooked chicken (optional)

Instructions:

1. Spread mayonnaise or cream cheese on one slice of bread.
2. Add a slice of cheese and layer with deli meat or chicken (if desired).
3. Use sliced veggies to create a "face" on the sandwich. For example, use olive slices for eyes, a cucumber slice for a nose, and a carrot slice for a mouth.
4. Serve as a fun and creative sandwich for kids and adults alike!

Frozen Yogurt Bark

Ingredients:

- 2 cups Greek yogurt (or regular yogurt)
- 2 tablespoons honey or maple syrup
- 1/2 cup mixed berries (blueberries, strawberries, raspberries)
- 1/4 cup chopped nuts (almonds, pistachios, or walnuts)
- 1/4 cup granola or coconut flakes (optional)

Instructions:

1. Line a baking sheet with parchment paper.
2. In a bowl, mix the yogurt with honey or maple syrup.
3. Spread the yogurt mixture evenly over the parchment paper to about 1/2-inch thickness.
4. Sprinkle with berries, nuts, granola, or coconut flakes.
5. Freeze for 3-4 hours or until the yogurt is firm.
6. Break into pieces and serve as a refreshing, healthy treat!

Mac and Cheese Cups

Ingredients:

- 2 cups cooked elbow macaroni
- 1 cup shredded cheddar cheese
- 1/2 cup milk
- 1 tablespoon butter
- 1 tablespoon flour
- 1/2 teaspoon garlic powder
- Salt and pepper, to taste
- 1/2 cup breadcrumbs (optional)
- 1 tablespoon chopped parsley (optional)

Instructions:

1. Preheat your oven to 350°F (175°C) and grease a muffin tin.
2. In a saucepan, melt butter over medium heat. Add flour and cook for 1 minute to form a roux.
3. Slowly add milk, whisking constantly to avoid lumps. Cook until the mixture thickens.
4. Stir in shredded cheese, garlic powder, salt, and pepper until smooth.
5. Add the cooked macaroni to the cheese sauce and stir until fully coated.
6. Spoon the mac and cheese into the muffin tin, filling each cup about 3/4 full. Top with breadcrumbs if desired.
7. Bake for 15-20 minutes, or until the tops are golden brown.
8. Let cool for a few minutes before serving. Garnish with chopped parsley if desired.

Fruit and Yogurt Parfaits

Ingredients:

- 1 cup Greek yogurt (or regular yogurt)
- 1 tablespoon honey or maple syrup
- 1/2 cup granola
- 1 cup mixed fresh fruit (strawberries, blueberries, bananas, etc.)
- Mint leaves (optional)

Instructions:

1. In a small bowl, mix the yogurt with honey or maple syrup.
2. In serving glasses or bowls, layer yogurt, granola, and fresh fruit.
3. Repeat the layers until the glasses are filled, ending with a layer of fruit on top.
4. Garnish with mint leaves if desired.
5. Serve immediately for a refreshing and healthy snack or breakfast.

Mini Frittatas

Ingredients:

- 6 eggs
- 1/4 cup milk
- 1/2 cup shredded cheese (cheddar, mozzarella, or your choice)
- 1/2 cup diced vegetables (bell peppers, onions, spinach, etc.)
- Salt and pepper, to taste
- 1 tablespoon olive oil (for greasing muffin tin)

Instructions:

1. Preheat your oven to 375°F (190°C) and grease a muffin tin with olive oil.
2. In a bowl, whisk together eggs, milk, salt, and pepper.
3. Stir in the shredded cheese and diced vegetables.
4. Pour the mixture evenly into the muffin tin cups, filling each about 3/4 full.
5. Bake for 15-20 minutes, or until the frittatas are set and lightly golden on top.
6. Let cool for a few minutes before serving. These can be enjoyed warm or cold!

Cinnamon Roll Bites

Ingredients:

- 1 can refrigerated cinnamon rolls (8-count)
- 2 tablespoons butter, melted
- 1/4 cup cinnamon sugar
- 1/4 cup icing (optional)

Instructions:

1. Preheat your oven to 375°F (190°C) and grease a mini muffin tin.
2. Unroll the cinnamon rolls and cut each roll into 4 smaller pieces.
3. Roll each piece in cinnamon sugar and place it into the muffin tin.
4. Drizzle the melted butter over the cinnamon roll bites.
5. Bake for 12-15 minutes, or until golden and puffed.
6. If desired, drizzle the included icing over the top before serving.

Mini Calzones

Ingredients:

- 1 package pizza dough (store-bought or homemade)
- 1 cup ricotta cheese
- 1/2 cup shredded mozzarella cheese
- 1/4 cup pepperoni or cooked sausage (optional)
- 1/4 cup marinara sauce
- 1 egg (for egg wash)
- Salt and pepper to taste

Instructions:

1. Preheat your oven to 375°F (190°C) and grease a baking sheet.
2. Roll out the pizza dough on a floured surface and cut it into 6-8 small circles.
3. In a bowl, combine the ricotta cheese, mozzarella, and optional fillings (pepperoni, sausage).
4. Spoon the cheese mixture onto the center of each dough circle.
5. Fold the dough over the filling and seal the edges by pinching.
6. Place the calzones on the baking sheet. Brush the tops with a beaten egg and sprinkle with salt and pepper.
7. Bake for 15-20 minutes, or until golden brown.
8. Serve with marinara sauce for dipping.

Carrot and Cucumber Rolls

Ingredients:

- 2 large carrots, peeled into thin ribbons
- 1 cucumber, peeled into thin ribbons
- 1/4 cup cream cheese (or hummus)
- Fresh dill or parsley for garnish (optional)

Instructions:

1. Use a vegetable peeler to make thin ribbons from the carrots and cucumber.
2. Spread a thin layer of cream cheese (or hummus) on each ribbon.
3. Gently roll up each vegetable ribbon and secure with a toothpick.
4. Garnish with fresh dill or parsley if desired.
5. Serve these fresh and crunchy rolls as a healthy snack.

Egg Salad Sandwiches

Ingredients:

- 4 boiled eggs, chopped
- 2 tablespoons mayonnaise
- 1 tablespoon mustard (optional)
- 1 tablespoon fresh dill or chives, chopped
- Salt and pepper, to taste
- 4 slices bread (white, whole wheat, or your choice)

Instructions:

1. In a bowl, combine the chopped eggs, mayonnaise, mustard, and fresh herbs.
2. Season with salt and pepper to taste.
3. Spread the egg salad onto slices of bread to make sandwiches.
4. Serve immediately, or cut into smaller finger sandwiches for easy serving.

Frozen Banana Bites

Ingredients:

- 2 ripe bananas, sliced
- 1/2 cup dark chocolate chips (or milk chocolate)
- 1 tablespoon coconut oil (optional)
- Crushed nuts or sprinkles (optional)

Instructions:

1. Slice the bananas into 1/2-inch thick rounds.
2. Melt the chocolate chips with coconut oil in a microwave-safe bowl, heating in 20-second intervals, stirring in between.
3. Dip each banana slice into the melted chocolate and place on a parchment-lined baking sheet.
4. Optionally, sprinkle with crushed nuts or sprinkles.
5. Freeze for 2 hours or until the chocolate hardens.
6. Serve as a refreshing and indulgent treat.

Rice Cake Snacks

Ingredients:

- 6 rice cakes
- 1/4 cup peanut butter or almond butter
- 1/4 cup honey or maple syrup
- Fresh fruit (sliced bananas, strawberries, or berries)
- Chopped nuts or granola (optional)

Instructions:

1. Spread a layer of peanut butter (or almond butter) on each rice cake.
2. Drizzle with honey or maple syrup for extra sweetness.
3. Top with fresh fruit slices and optional nuts or granola.
4. Serve as a healthy and satisfying snack.

Cheese and Crackers Art

Ingredients:

- Assorted crackers (e.g., whole-grain, sesame, or rye)
- Sliced cheeses (cheddar, gouda, swiss, etc.)
- Fresh fruits (e.g., grapes, apple slices, berries)
- Nuts (optional)
- Fresh herbs for garnish (e.g., rosemary or mint)

Instructions:

1. Arrange the crackers on a large platter in a decorative pattern.
2. Layer cheese slices on top of the crackers or on the side for variety.
3. Add fruits and nuts around the edges for pops of color and texture.
4. Garnish with fresh herbs to create a vibrant, edible "art piece."
5. Serve as a snack or party appetizer.

Veggie Pancakes

Ingredients:

- 1 cup shredded zucchini or carrots
- 1/4 cup chopped onion
- 2 eggs
- 1/4 cup flour (all-purpose or almond flour)
- 1/4 teaspoon baking powder
- Salt and pepper, to taste
- 2 tablespoons olive oil for frying

Instructions:

1. In a bowl, mix shredded veggies, onion, eggs, flour, baking powder, salt, and pepper until combined.
2. Heat olive oil in a non-stick pan over medium heat.
3. Scoop small portions of the batter into the pan and flatten slightly.
4. Cook for 2-3 minutes on each side until golden brown and crispy.
5. Serve warm with sour cream or yogurt as a topping.

Breakfast Burritos

Ingredients:

- 4 large tortillas
- 4 eggs, scrambled
- 1 cup cooked breakfast sausage or bacon pieces
- 1/2 cup shredded cheese
- 1/4 cup salsa or diced tomatoes
- 1/2 cup sautéed veggies (e.g., peppers and onions)

Instructions:

1. Lay each tortilla flat and fill with scrambled eggs, sausage, cheese, veggies, and salsa.
2. Fold in the sides of the tortilla and roll tightly.
3. Heat a skillet and place the burrito seam-side down for 2 minutes to seal.
4. Serve immediately or wrap in foil for an on-the-go breakfast.

Apple Cinnamon Oatmeal

Ingredients:

- 1 cup rolled oats
- 2 cups water or milk
- 1 apple, diced
- 1/2 teaspoon cinnamon
- 1 tablespoon honey or brown sugar
- Optional toppings: nuts, raisins, or maple syrup

Instructions:

1. In a saucepan, bring water or milk to a boil.
2. Add oats, diced apple, and cinnamon, stirring well.
3. Lower the heat and cook for 5-7 minutes, stirring occasionally.
4. Sweeten with honey or brown sugar, if desired.
5. Serve warm, topped with nuts or raisins for added texture.

Chocolate Rice Krispies Treats

Ingredients:

- 3 cups puffed rice cereal
- 1/4 cup cocoa powder
- 1/2 cup honey or syrup
- 1/4 cup peanut butter (optional)
- 1/4 cup chocolate chips (optional)

Instructions:

1. In a saucepan over low heat, combine honey, cocoa powder, and peanut butter until smooth.
2. Remove from heat and mix in the rice cereal until fully coated.
3. Press the mixture into a greased or lined pan.
4. Sprinkle with chocolate chips if desired.
5. Refrigerate for 1 hour before cutting into squares.

DIY Ice Cream Cones

Ingredients:

- Store-bought or homemade waffle cones
- 2 cups ice cream (any flavor)
- Sprinkles, crushed nuts, or chocolate chips for topping

Instructions:

1. Fill each cone with a scoop or two of your favorite ice cream.
2. Roll the top of the ice cream in sprinkles, nuts, or chocolate chips.
3. Serve immediately for a fun, customizable treat.

Homemade Pudding Cups

Ingredients:

- 2 cups milk
- 1/3 cup sugar
- 1/4 cup cocoa powder (for chocolate pudding) or vanilla extract (for vanilla pudding)
- 2 tablespoons cornstarch
- Pinch of salt

Instructions:

1. In a saucepan, whisk together sugar, cocoa powder (or vanilla), cornstarch, and salt.
2. Gradually add milk, whisking to combine.
3. Cook over medium heat, stirring constantly, until the mixture thickens (about 5-7 minutes).
4. Pour into small cups or bowls and refrigerate for 2 hours.
5. Serve with whipped cream or fresh fruit on top.

Pita Bread Pizzas

Ingredients:

- 4 pita breads
- 1/2 cup marinara or pizza sauce
- 1 cup shredded mozzarella cheese
- Toppings: sliced pepperoni, veggies, olives, etc.

Instructions:

1. Preheat oven to 375°F (190°C).
2. Spread marinara sauce evenly on each pita bread.
3. Sprinkle cheese on top, followed by your desired toppings.
4. Bake on a baking sheet for 10-12 minutes, or until the cheese is melted and bubbly.
5. Serve immediately as a quick and delicious meal.

Fruit and Cheese Kabobs

Ingredients:

- Assorted fresh fruits (e.g., grapes, strawberries, pineapple, apple chunks)
- Cubed cheese (cheddar, gouda, or mozzarella)
- Skewers

Instructions:

1. Alternate threading fruits and cheese cubes onto the skewers.
2. Arrange on a platter for serving.
3. Optional: Drizzle with honey or sprinkle with cinnamon for added flavor.

Sweet Potato and Apple Hash

Ingredients:

- 2 medium sweet potatoes, diced
- 1 apple, diced
- 1/2 onion, chopped
- 2 tablespoons olive oil
- 1 teaspoon cinnamon
- Salt and pepper, to taste

Instructions:

1. Heat olive oil in a skillet over medium heat.
2. Add sweet potatoes and cook for 5-7 minutes, stirring occasionally.
3. Add onion and apple, then sprinkle with cinnamon, salt, and pepper.
4. Cook for another 5 minutes or until tender.
5. Serve warm as a side dish or breakfast option.

Spinach and Cheese Pinwheels

Ingredients:

- 1 sheet puff pastry, thawed
- 1 cup fresh spinach, chopped
- 1/2 cup shredded cheese (cheddar or mozzarella)
- 1 egg, beaten

Instructions:

1. Preheat oven to 375°F (190°C).
2. Roll out the puff pastry and spread chopped spinach and cheese evenly over it.
3. Roll the pastry into a log and slice into 1-inch pieces.
4. Place slices on a baking sheet lined with parchment paper.
5. Brush with beaten egg and bake for 15-20 minutes, or until golden brown.

Popcorn Trail Mix

Ingredients:

- 3 cups popped popcorn
- 1/2 cup nuts (almonds, peanuts, or cashews)
- 1/2 cup dried fruit (raisins, cranberries, or apricots)
- 1/4 cup chocolate chips (optional)

Instructions:

1. In a large bowl, combine popcorn, nuts, dried fruit, and chocolate chips.
2. Toss to mix evenly.
3. Serve as a quick and portable snack.

Mini Bagel Pizzas

Ingredients:

- 4 mini bagels, sliced in half
- 1/2 cup pizza sauce
- 1 cup shredded mozzarella cheese
- Optional toppings: pepperoni, veggies, or olives

Instructions:

1. Preheat oven to 375°F (190°C).
2. Spread pizza sauce over each bagel half.
3. Sprinkle with cheese and add desired toppings.
4. Place on a baking sheet and bake for 8-10 minutes, or until cheese is melted.

Fruit Smoothies

Ingredients:

- 1 cup fresh or frozen fruit (e.g., berries, mango, banana)
- 1 cup yogurt or milk (dairy or plant-based)
- 1 tablespoon honey or maple syrup (optional)
- Ice cubes (optional)

Instructions:

1. Combine all ingredients in a blender.
2. Blend until smooth.
3. Pour into a glass and serve immediately.

Veggie and Cheese Muffins

Ingredients:

- 1 cup shredded zucchini or carrots
- 1 cup flour (all-purpose or whole wheat)
- 1/2 teaspoon baking powder
- 1/2 cup shredded cheese (cheddar or parmesan)
- 1/4 cup milk
- 1 egg
- 2 tablespoons olive oil
- Salt and pepper, to taste

Instructions:

1. Preheat oven to 375°F (190°C) and grease a muffin tin.
2. In a bowl, mix flour, baking powder, salt, and pepper.
3. Add shredded veggies and cheese.
4. In a separate bowl, whisk milk, egg, and olive oil, then combine with dry ingredients.
5. Spoon the batter into the muffin tin, filling each cup about 3/4 full.
6. Bake for 18-20 minutes, or until a toothpick comes out clean.

www.ingramcontent.com/pod-product-compliance
Lightning Source LLC
LaVergne TN
LVHW081509060526
838201LV00056BA/3020